VOL. IV
ILLUMINATION

PERSONAL ILLUMINATIONS

MY SPIRITUAL JOURNAL

JAMES C. CHRISTENSEN

PERSONAL ILLUMINATIONS

VOL. IV
ILLUMINATION

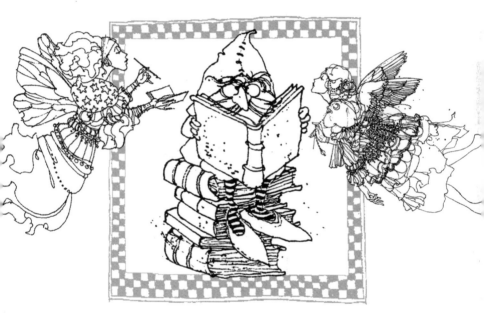

SHADOW
MOUNTAIN

ISBN 1-57345-858-9

OTHER BOOKS IN THE PERSONAL ILLUMINATIONS SERIES:

Imagination: My Creative Journal
Exploration: My Travel Journal
Enumeration: My Book of Lists
The Personal Illuminations Journal (hardcover)

Designed by Peter Landa and Milly Iacono
Printed in the United States of America

10 9 8 7 6 5 4 3 2 1

INTRODUCTION

JAMES C. CHRISTENSEN

Of all the journals in the Personal Illuminations series, this volume might very well be the most "personally illuminating" once you have filled it. It contains thoughts and sayings that have inspired me on my own spiritual journey. I use my journals to record things that I want to remember later—feelings, events, and reactions to my experiences. I also write down quotes or phrases I hear in church talks, or at the dinner table, or even things I overhear in public places. You never know when you'll hear something that expresses an idea in just the right way.

I can go back to my journals years later to remind myself of these important ideas. And, since I am primarily a visual artist, most of my pages have doodles and sketches of what I have been thinking about. You can doodle in this journal, too. You don't need a degree in art to draw in your journal.

Words and pictures—both create the historical document of our lives. As you fill this book with your thoughts and favorite quotations or scriptures, it can become your friend—both a comfort and an inspiration to you.

James Christensen

BEGIN TODAY! NO MATTER HOW FEEBLE THE LIGHT, LET IT SHINE AS BEST IT MAY. THE WORLD MAY NEED JUST THAT QUALITY OF LIGHT WHICH YOU HAVE.   ~SHAKER SAYING

THE GREATEST BLESSINGS THE LORD HAS FOR US ARE IN THE SECOND MILE.

"Too many people are trying to serve the Lord without offending the devil."
~ Robert Millet

"WE DO NOT NEED TO BE QUALIFIED. THE GIFT OF LOVE IS FREE, BUT WE MUST PRACTICE." ~MADELEINE L'ENGLE

SIN IS KNOWING THE WILL OF GOD AND NOT DOING IT.

WHEN the SPIRIT STRIVES WITH US

1. WE ARE NOT EASILY OFFENDED.

2. WE FEEL CONFIDENT IN WHAT WE DO.

3. WE ARE HAPPY AND CALM.

4. OUR MINDS ARE CLEAR AND FULL OF LIGHT.

5. WE ARE GENEROUS.

6. WE ARE GLAD WHEN OTHERS SUCCEED.

7. WE WANT TO MAKE OTHERS HAPPY AND BRING OUT THE BEST IN THEM.

8. WE FEEL LIKE PRAYING.

9. WE ARE MORE SERENE IN DIFFICULT TIMES.

10. WE OVERCOME TEMPTATIONS.

A TRUE CHRISTIAN CAN HAVE
OPPONENTS BUT NEVER
ENEMIES.

THE MORE YOU COMPLAIN,
THE LONGER
GOD LETS YOU LIVE.

IF WE WERE ARRESTED AND PUT ON TRIAL FOR BEING A CHRISTIAN, WOULD THERE BE ENOUGH EVIDENCE TO CONVICT US?

Too often we live
the Gospel through
clenched
teeth. — MT

SOMETIMES THE SPIRIT TOUCHES US THROUGH OUR WEAKNESSES.

SOLE SEARCHING

WE DO NOT LIKE
THE WORDS:
SUBMIT
SURRENDER
YET THAT IS WHAT WE
MUST DO TO CONQUER

THE MAN ON TOP OF THE MOUNTAIN DIDN'T FALL THERE

PART OF WHY WE'RE HERE IS TO LEARN TO BE NICE TO EACH OTHER.

ACCEPTANCE WITHOUT PROOF IS THE FUNDAMENTAL CHARACTERISTIC OF RELIGION. REJECTION WITHOUT PROOF IS THE FUNDAMENTAL CHARACTERISTIC OF WESTERN SCIENCE.

"IF MY RELIGION IS TRUE, IT WILL STAND UP TO ALL MY QUESTIONING; THERE IS NO FEAR." ~MADELEINE L'ENGLE

WILL THERE BE DAY PLANNERS IN HEAVEN?

THE LORD IS MORE INTERESTED IN OUR
AVAILABILITY THAN IN OUR CAPABILITY
BECAUSE HE KNOWS OUR POSSIBILITIES.

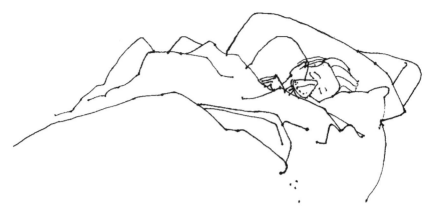

"I'M NOT AFRAID OF DYING, IT'S JUST THE PROCESS OF GETTING DEAD THAT I'M NOT CRAZY ABOUT."   ~MAY DEWITT

WE ARE SPIRITUAL BEINGS PRACTICING MORTALITY

...NOT MORTALS PRACTICING SPIRITUALITY.

IF YOU'RE GOING TO DINE WITH THE DEVIL,
YOU'D BETTER USE A LONG SPOON.

IF YOU PRAY FOR STRENGTH, GOD SENDS YOU A SET OF WEIGHTS.

"If we live in the Spirit, let us also walk in the Spirit."

~GALATIANS 5:25

GOD LOVES YOU JUST THE WAY
YOU ARE,
BUT HE LOVES YOU TOO MUCH
TO LEAVE YOU THAT WAY.

LABOR TO MAKE THE WAY OF GOD
YOUR OWN; LET IT BE YOUR INHERITANCE,
YOUR TREASURE, YOUR OCCUPATION,
YOUR DAILY CALLING.   ~SHAKER SAYING

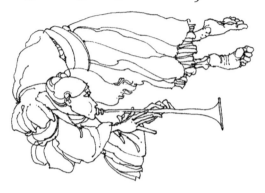

THE SMARTEST THING THAT SATAN HAS DONE IS TO CONVINCE MAN THAT HE DOES NOT EXIST.

"I LIFT THEE AND THEE LIFT ME, AND WE LASCEND TOGETHER." ~QUAKER PROVERB

THE ONLY BURDENS THAT ARE TOO HEAVY TO BEAR ARE THE ONES WE TRY TO CARRY ALONE.

IF IT'S FAIR, IT'S
NOT A TRIAL.

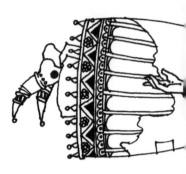

"LORD, I BELIEVE; HELP THOU MINE UNBELIEF." ~MARK 9:24

He deserves
Paradise
who makes his
companions laugh.
~The Koran

"IT IS ONE OF THE GREATER TRIUMPHS OF
LUCIFER THAT HE HAS MANAGED TO MAKE
CHRISTIANS BELIEVE THAT A STORY IS A LIE,
THAT A MYTH SHOULD BE OUTGROWN..."
~MADELEINE L'ENGLE

"GOD'S GIFT OF THE WORLD OBLIGES US TO PROTECT IT AND CARE FOR IT. MAN'S DOMINION IS A CALL TO SERVICE, NOT A LICENSE TO EXTERMINATE." ~HUGH NIBLEY

KEEP BUSY. IDLENESS IS THE STRENGTH OF BAD HABITS.   ~ SHAKER SAYING

GOD MUST HAVE A SENSE OF HUMOR, OTHERWISE SOME OF US WOULDN'T BE HERE.

OFTEN THE LORD DOES NOT LIGHT THE WHOLE PATH, BUT REQUIRES US TO HAVE THE FAITH TO TAKE A STEP INTO THE DARKNESS, TO FIND THAT THE NEXT STEP BECOMES LIGHTED. ■ STEP BY STEP WE TEST OUR FAITH AND THE WAY IS PREPARED FOR US. ■ IF WE COULD SEE THE END FROM THE BEGINNING, IT WOULD NOT REQUIRE FAITH, AND OUR LIVES WOULD NOT BE A TEST OF FAITH.

VISION WITHOUT ACTION
IS MERELY A DREAM.

ACTION WITHOUT VISION
JUST PASSES THE TIME.

VISION WITH ACTION
CAN CHANGE THE WORLD.